Smart Word Tracing For Children

Kindergarten

by Elite Schooler Workbooks

Important Legal Information:

This workbook contains reproducibles. These are worksheets designed with the goal of being photocopied as much as required. Accordingly, I grant you the non-commercial right to photocopy any part of this workbook for any non-commercial, or educational, use.

All further rights are reserved © 2019.

ISBN: 9781704000336

Dolch Kindergarten Sight Words

All / all	Do / do	No / no	She / she	Well / well
Am / am	Eat / eat	Now / now	So / so	Went / went
Are / are	Four / four	On / on	Soon / soon	What / what
At / at	Get / get	Our / our	That / that	White / white
Ate / ate	Good / good	Out / out	There / there	Who / who
Be / be	Have / have	Please / please	They / they	Will / will
Black / black	He / he	Pretty / pretty	This / this	With / with
Brown / brown	Into / into	Ran / ran	Too / too	Yes / yes
But / but	Like / like	Ride / ride	Under / under	
Came / came	Must / must	Saw / saw	Want / want	
Did / did	New / new	Say / say	Was / was	

Instructions For The Educator

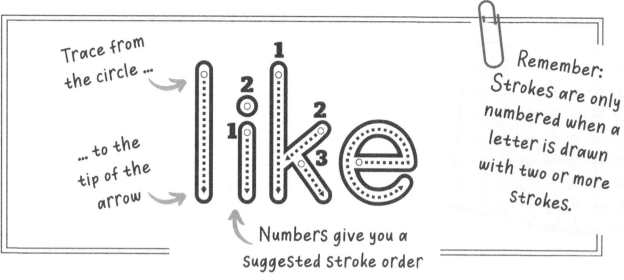

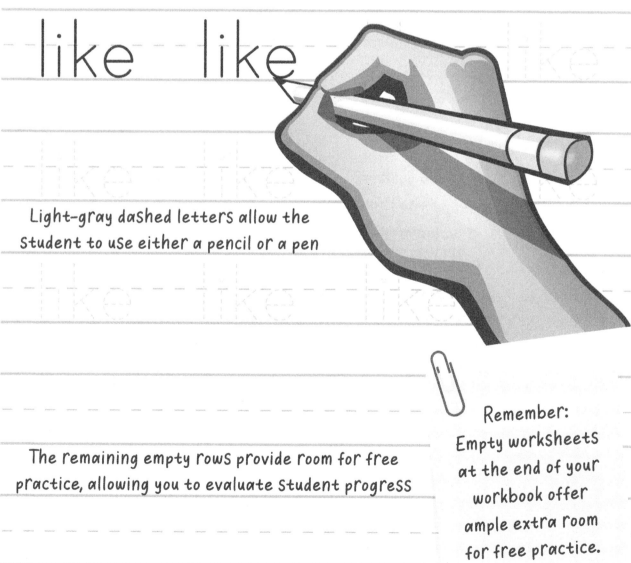

How To Use The Empty Worksheets

Simply write the desired word on the white box

If you wish to extend the lifetime value of your workbook make sure to copy the empty worksheet before writing on it.

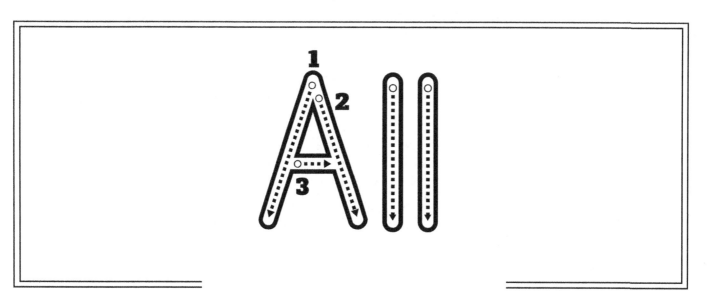

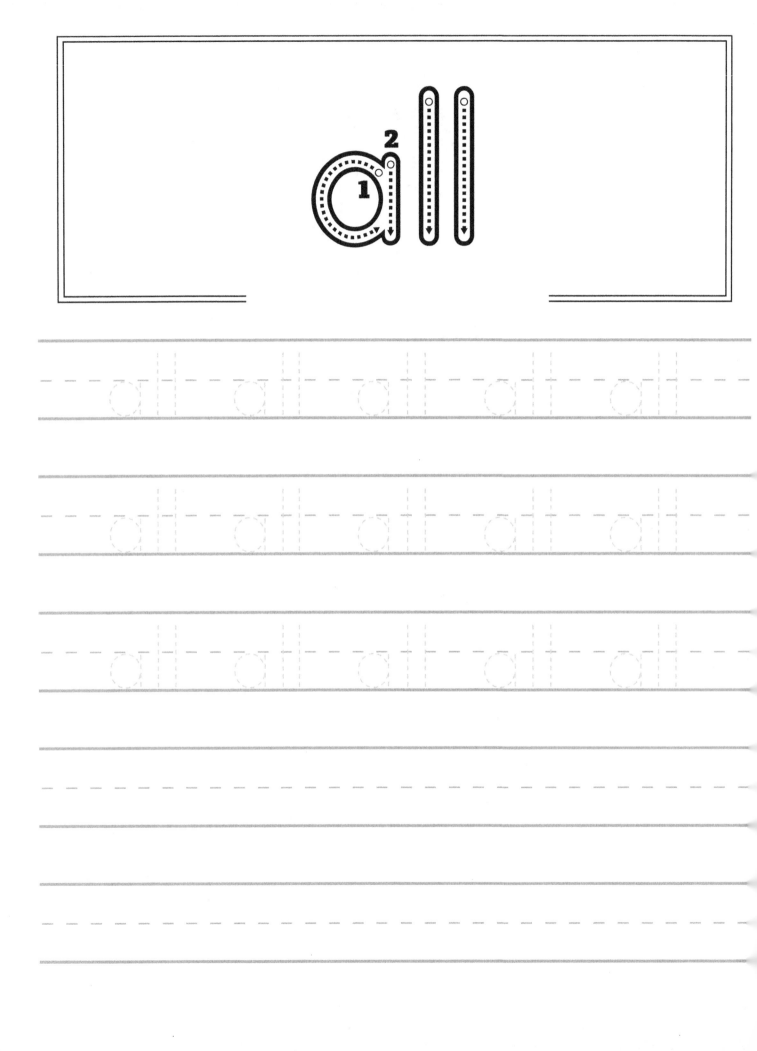

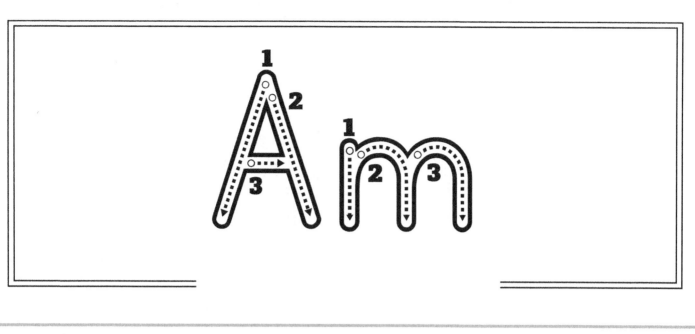

Am Am Am Am

Am Am Am Am

Am Am Am Am

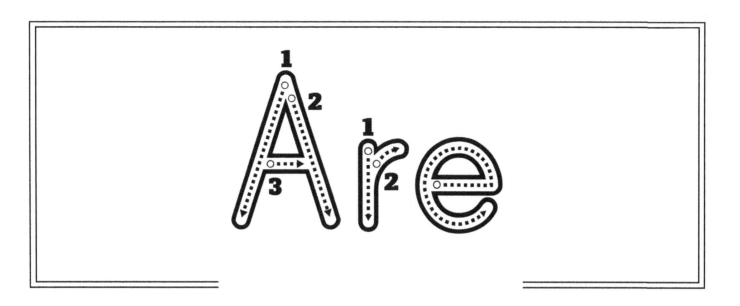

Are Are Are Are

Are Are Are Are

Are Are Are Are

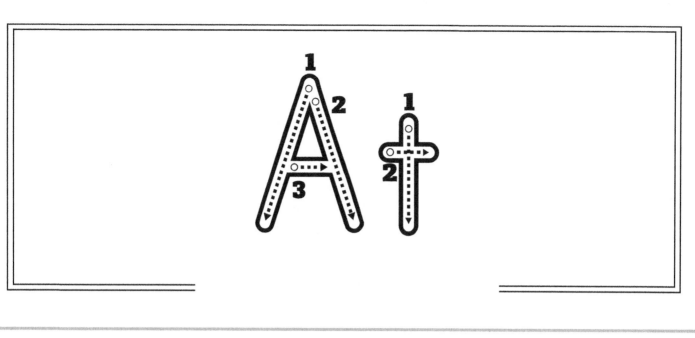

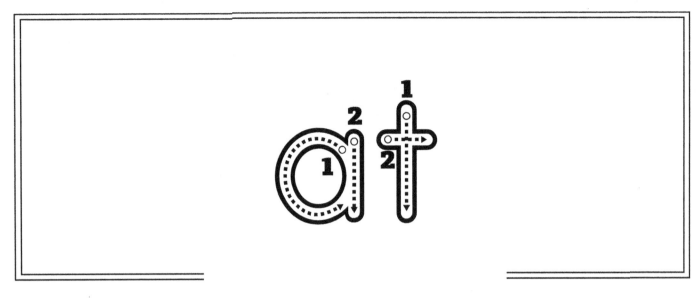

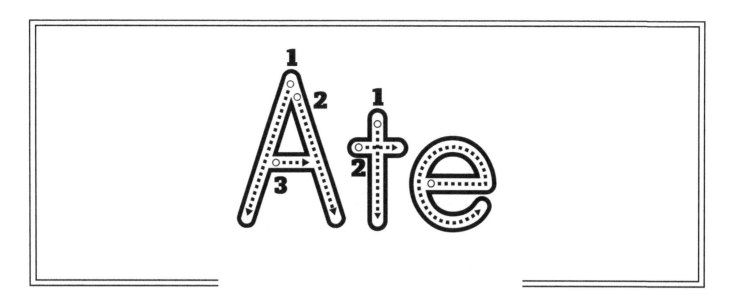

Ate Ate Ate Ate

Ate Ate Ate Ate

Ate Ate Ate Ate

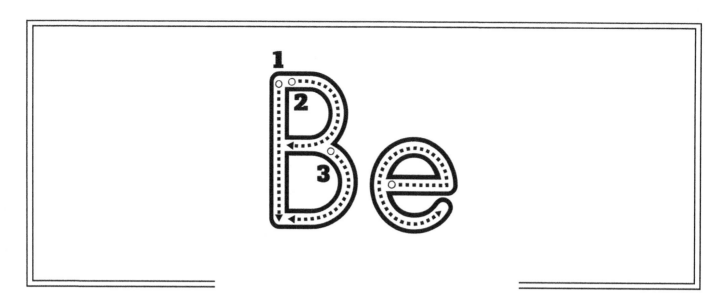

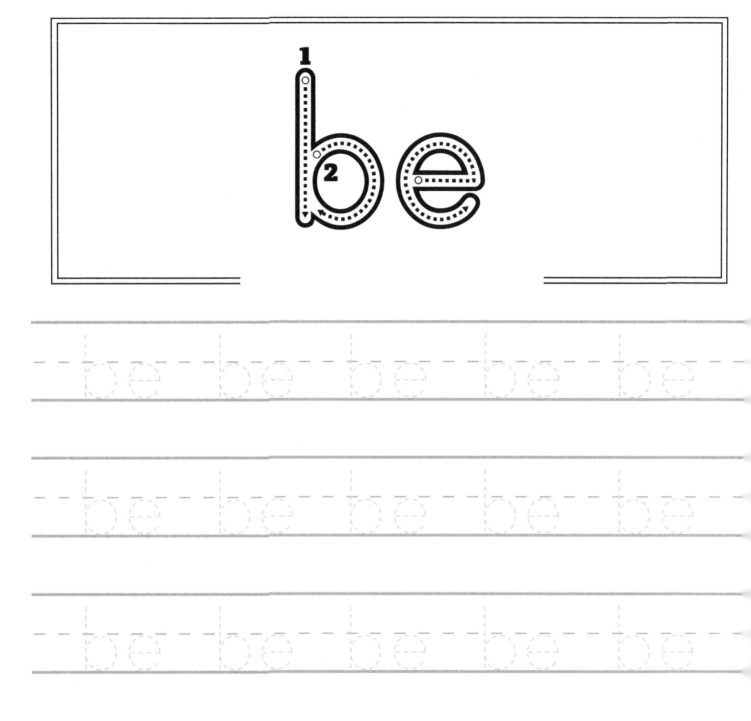

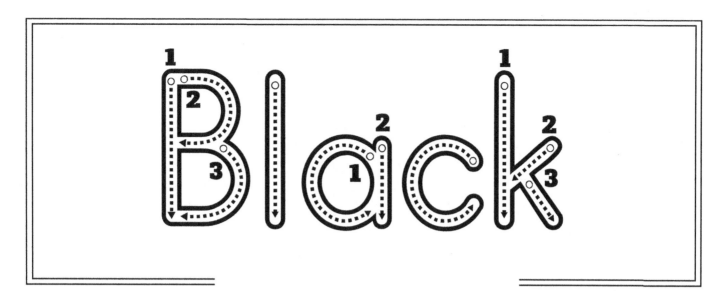

Black   Black   Black

Black   Black   Black

Black   Black   Black

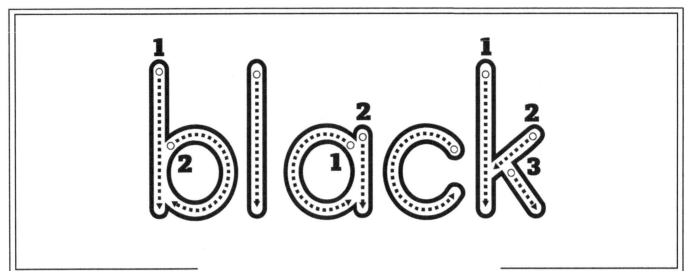

black　　black　　black

black　　black　　black

black　　black　　black

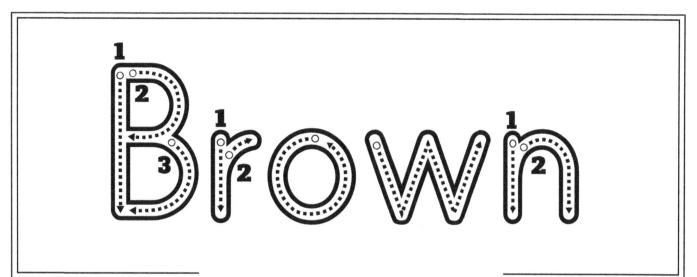

Brown   Brown

Brown   Brown

Brown   Brown

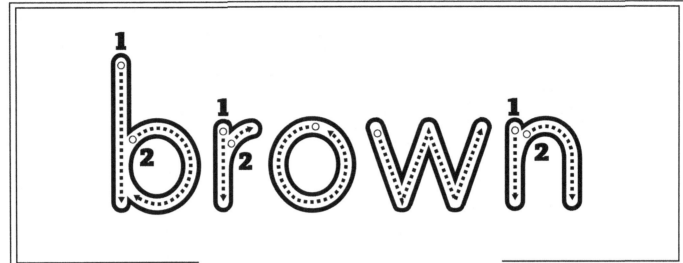

brown   brown

brown   brown

brown   brown

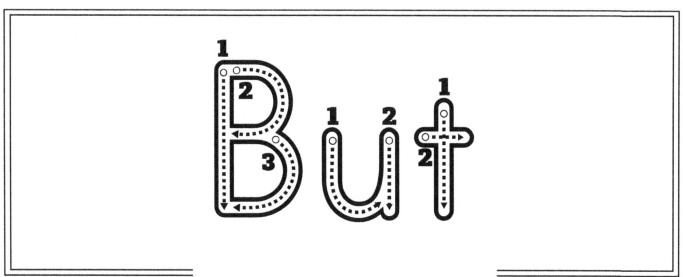

But But But But

But But But But

But But But But

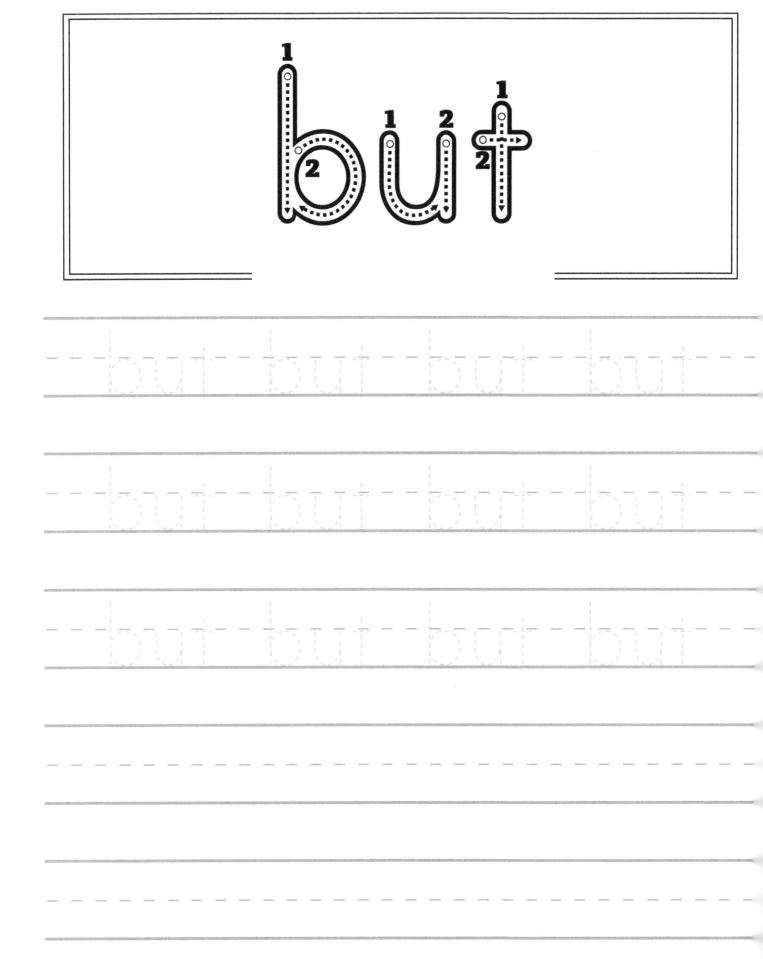

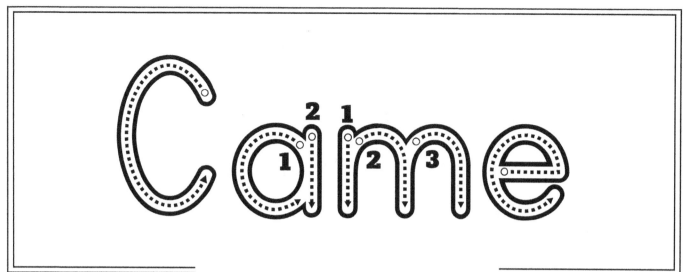

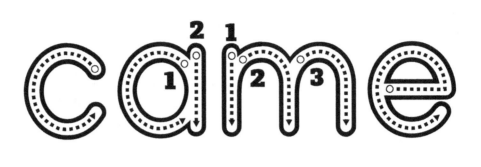

came came came

came came came

came came came

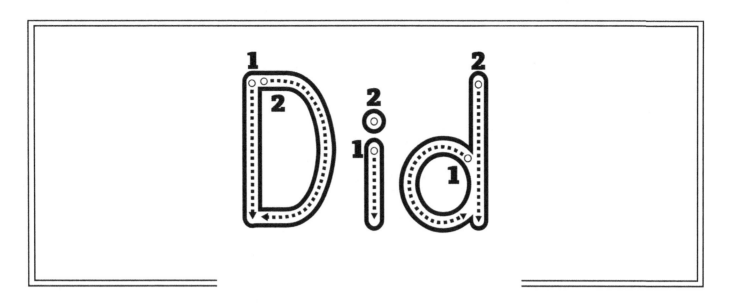

Did Did Did Did

Did Did Did Did

Did Did Did Did

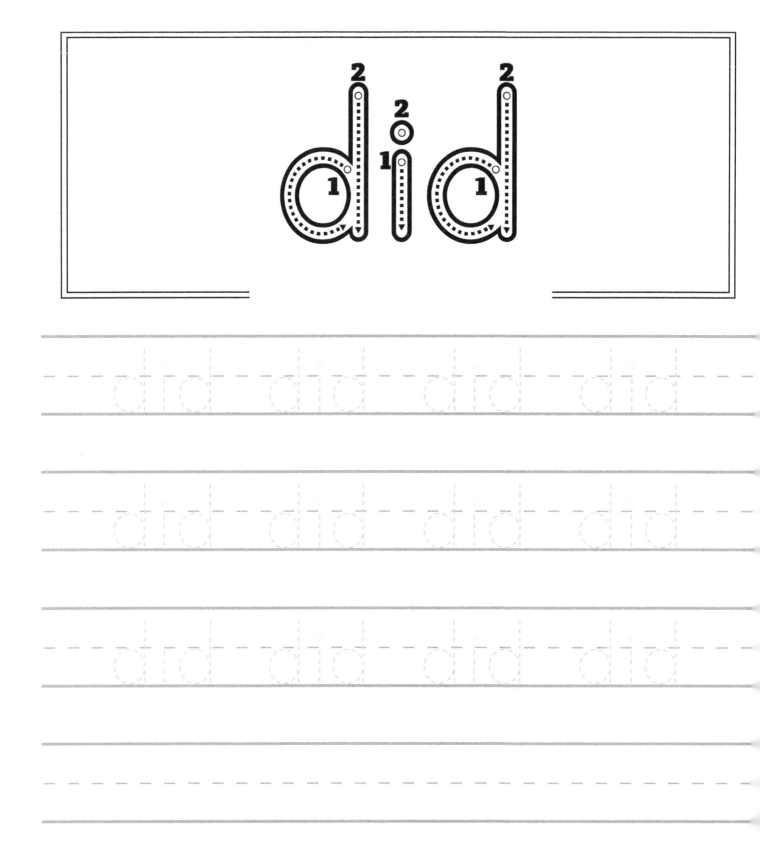

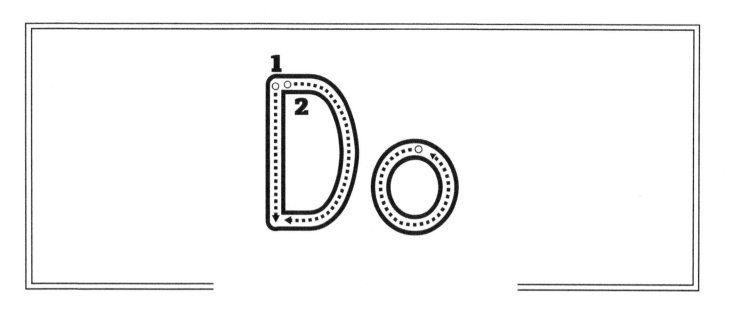

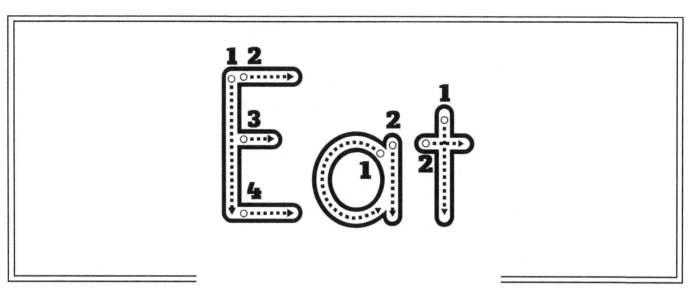

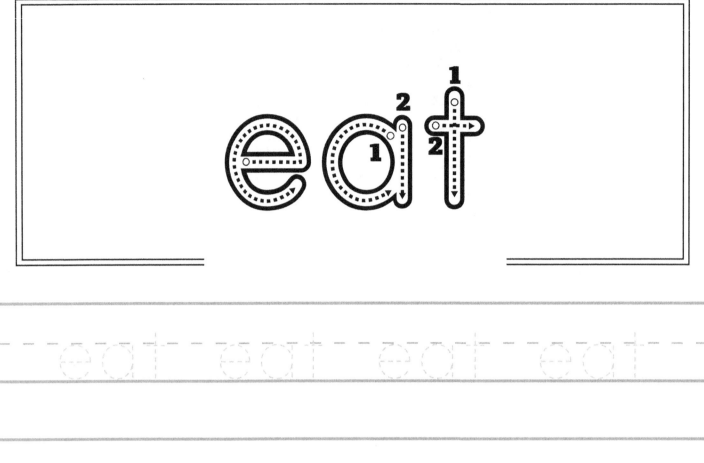

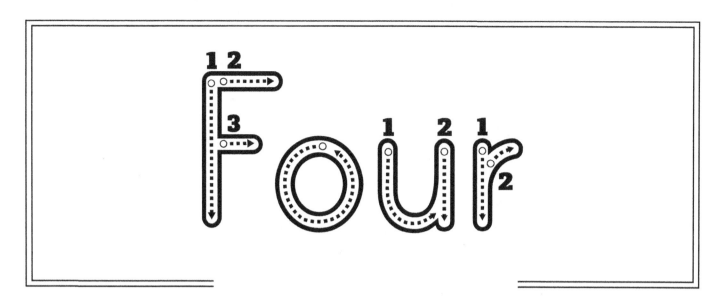

Four Four Four

Four Four Four

Four Four Four

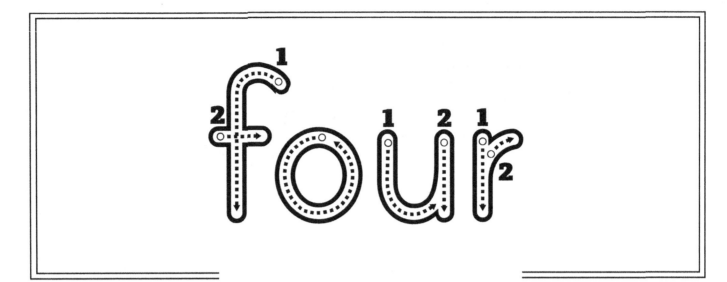

four   four   four

four   four   four

four   four   four

Get Get Get Get

Get Get Get Get

Get Get Get Get

Good

Good Good Good

Good Good Good

Good Good Good

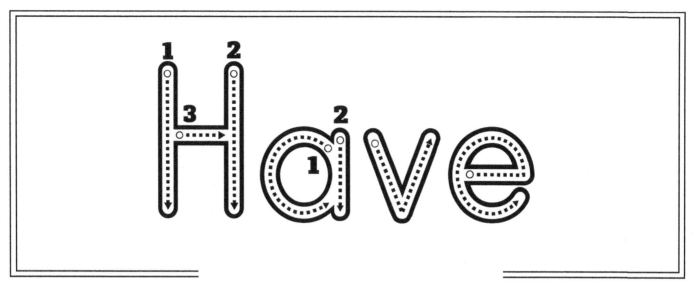

Have   Have   Have

Have   Have   Have

Have   Have   Have

have   have   have

have   have   have

have   have   have

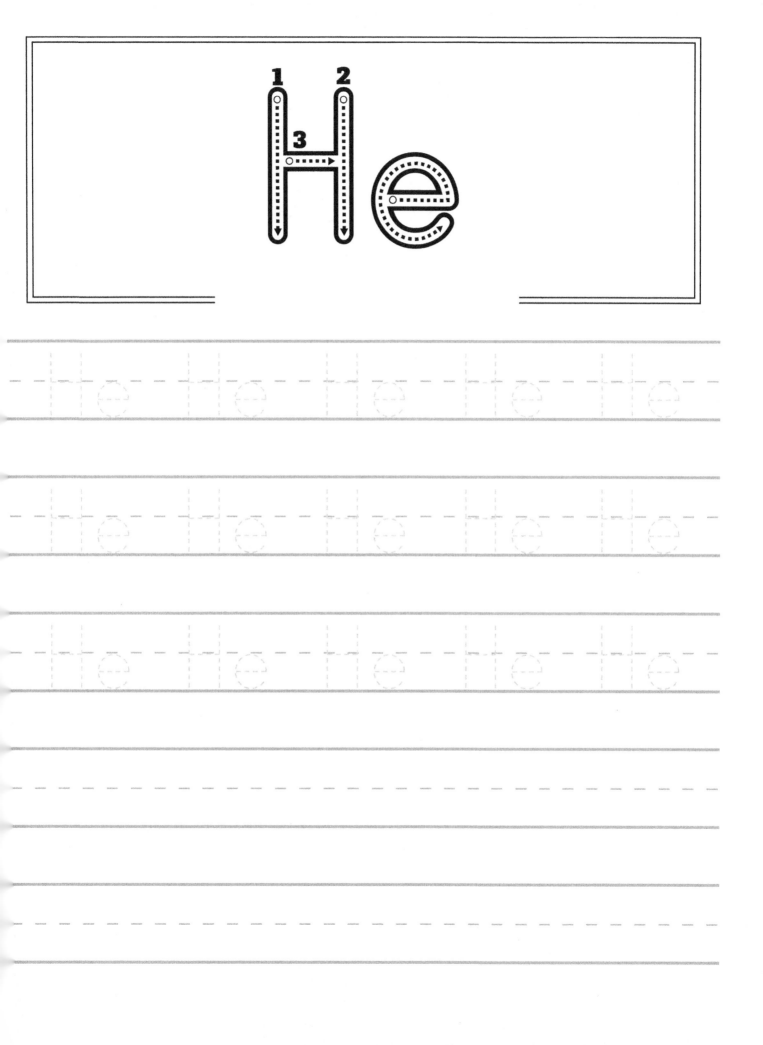

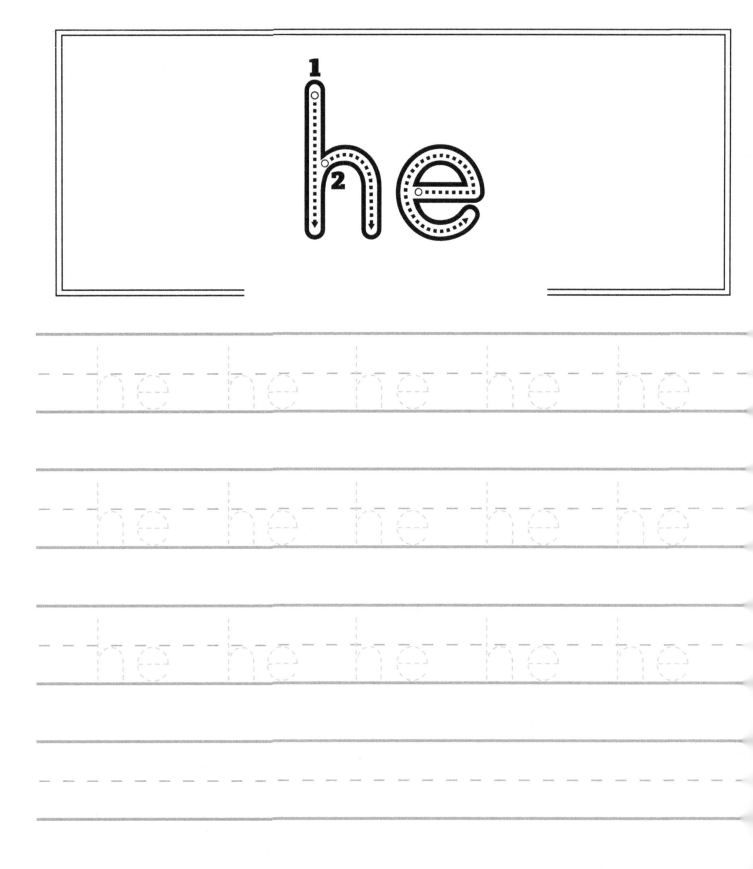

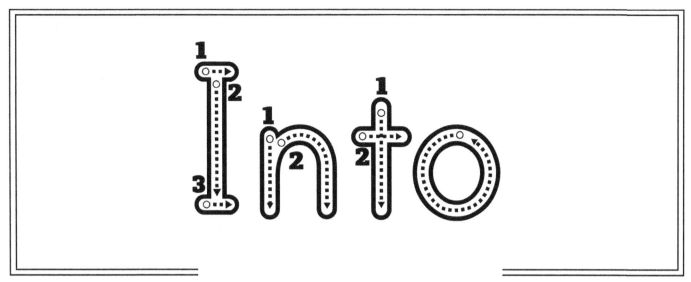

Into   Into   Into

Into   Into   Into

Into   Into   Into

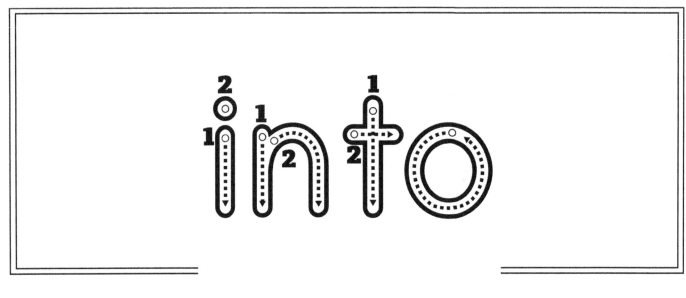

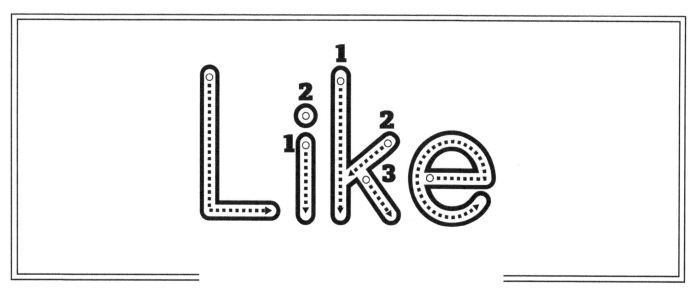

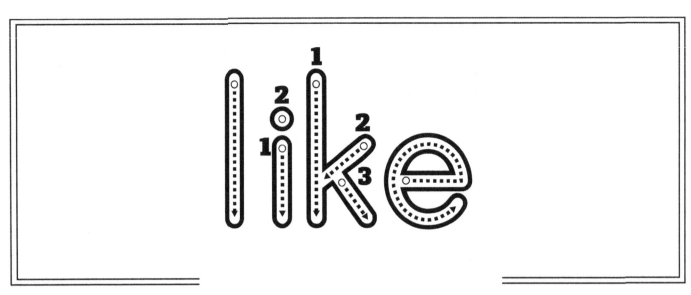

Must

Must Must Must

Must Must Must

Must Must Must

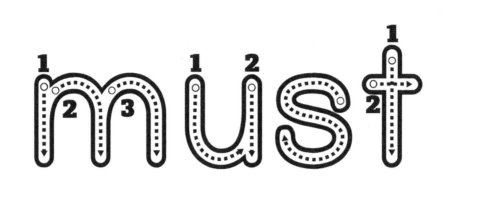

must   must   must

must   must   must

must   must   must

New New New

New New New

New New New

new new new

new new new

new new new

Now

Now Now Now

Now Now Now

Now Now Now

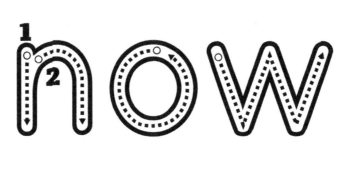

now now now

now now now

now now now

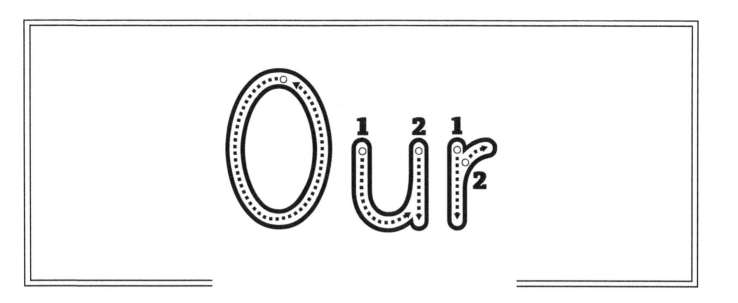

Our   Our   Our   Our

Our   Our   Our   Our

Our   Our   Our   Our

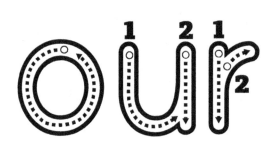

our our our our

our our our our

our our our our

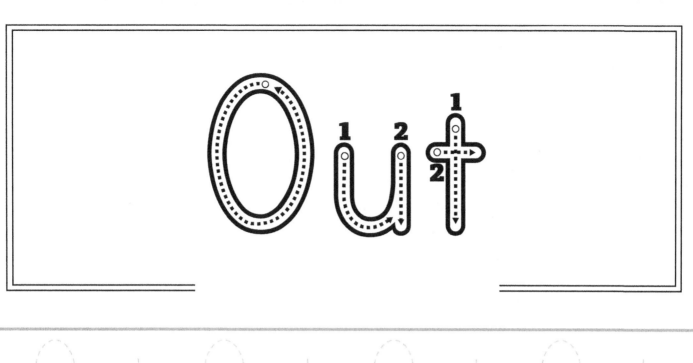

Out   Out   Out   Out

Out   Out   Out   Out

Out   Out   Out   Out

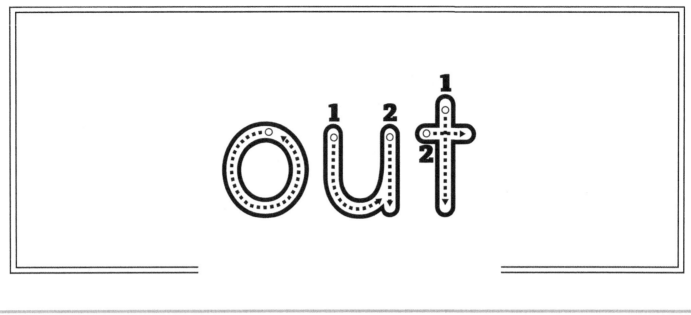

out out out out

out out out out

out out out out

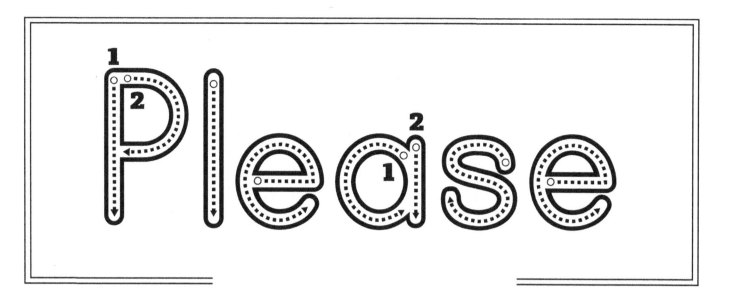

Please   Please

Please   Please

Please   Please

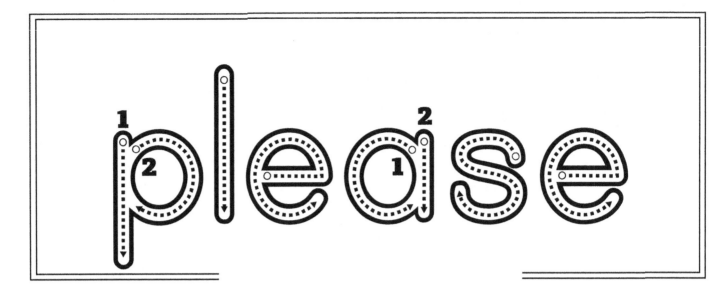

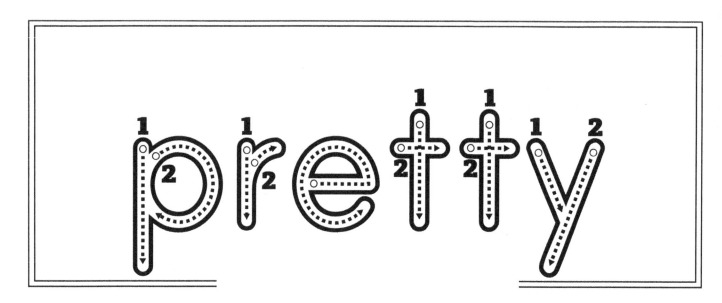

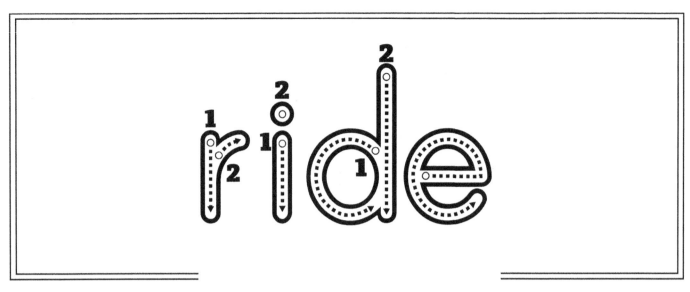

Saw

Saw   Saw   Saw

Saw   Saw   Saw

Saw   Saw   Saw

saw

saw   saw   saw

saw   saw   saw

saw   saw   saw

Say

Say Say Say Say

Say Say Say Say

Say Say Say Say

say

say say say say

say say say say

say say say say

She

She She She She

She She She She

She She She She

Soon

Soon   Soon   Soon

Soon   Soon   Soon

Soon   Soon   Soon

soon

soon   soon   soon

soon   soon   soon

soon   soon   soon

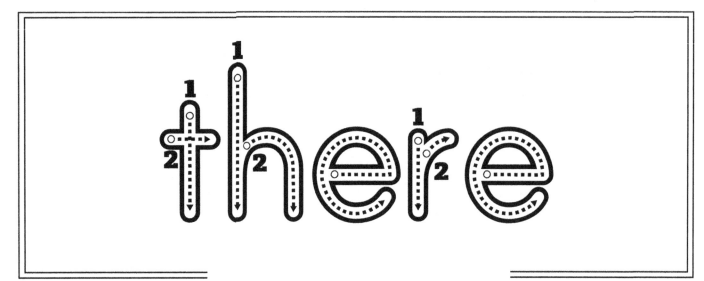

there   there   there

there   there   there

there   there   there

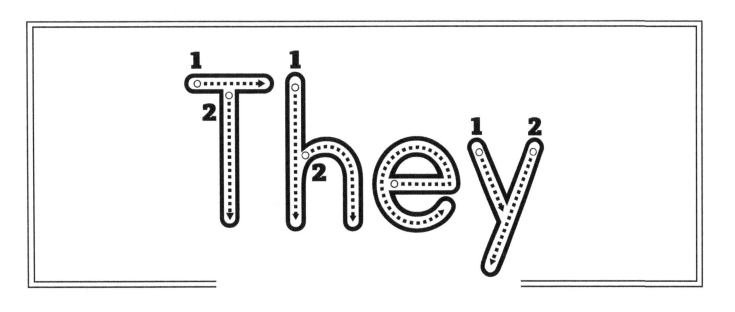

They   They   They

They   They   They

They   They   They

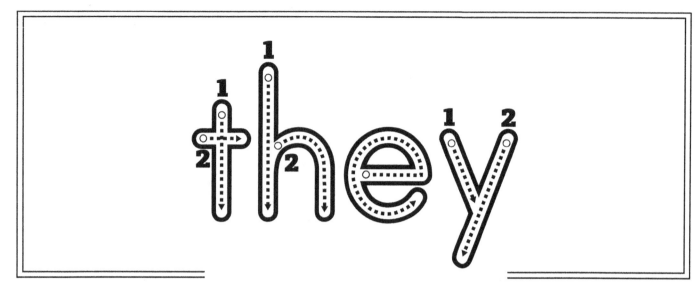

they they they

they they they

they they they

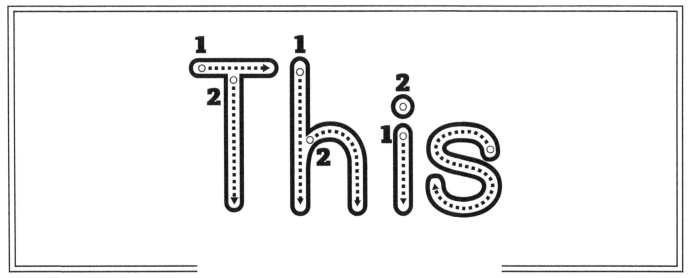

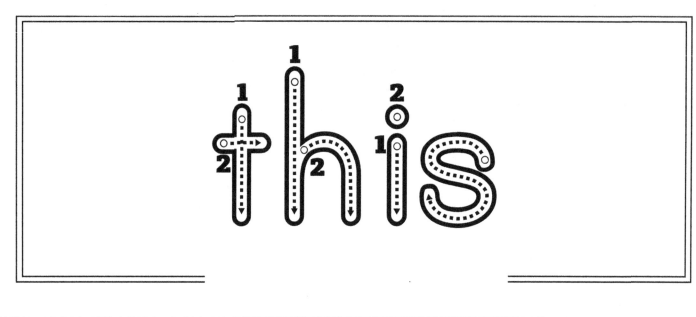

this this this this

this this this this

this this this this

too   too   too   too

too   too   too   too

too   too   too   too

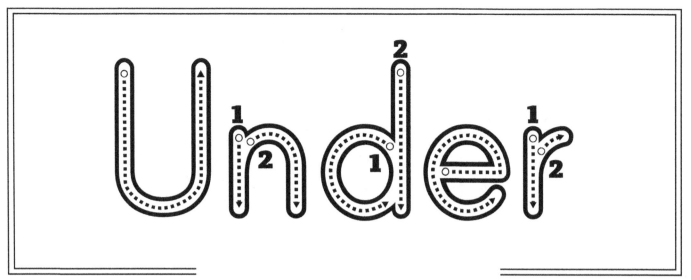

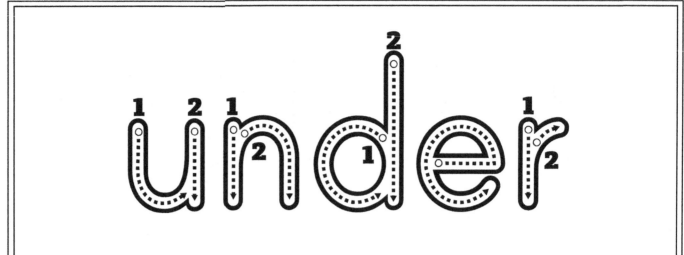

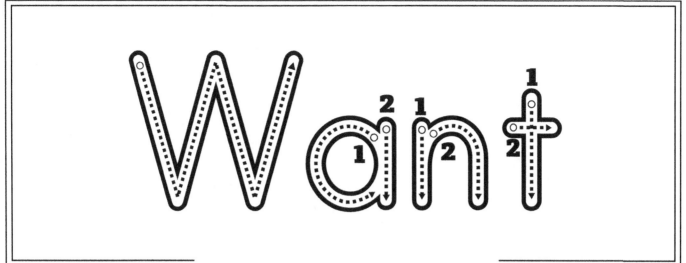

Want   Want   Want

Want   Want   Want

Want   Want   Want

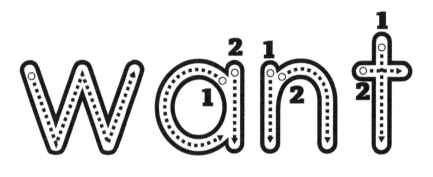

Was

Was   Was   Was

Was   Was   Was

Was   Was   Was

was

was   was   was

was   was   was

was   was   was

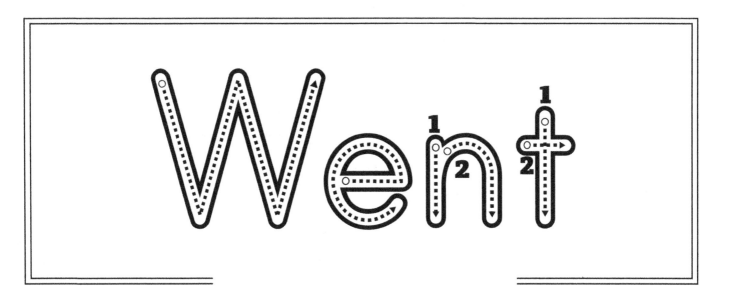

Went Went Went

Went Went Went

Went Went Went

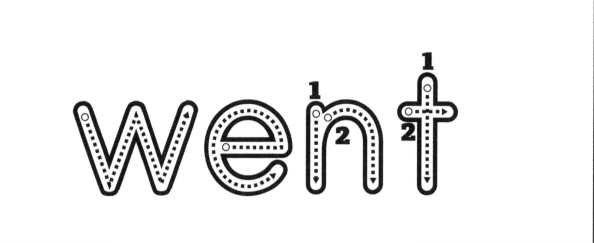

went went went

went went went

went went went

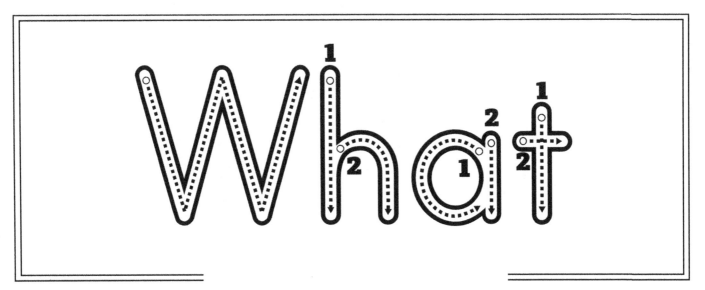

What What What

What What What

What What What

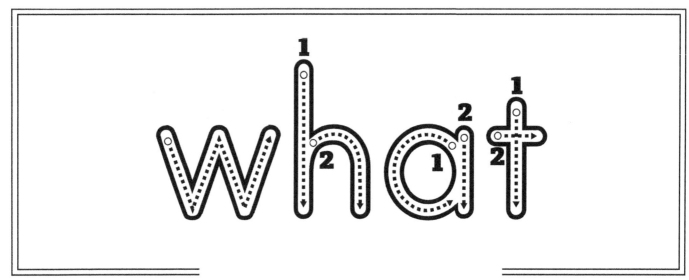

what   what   what

what   what   what

what   what   what

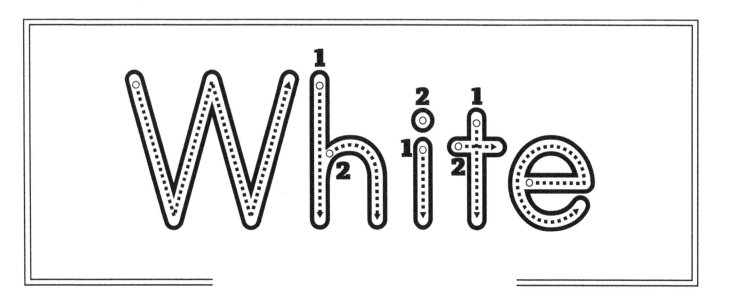

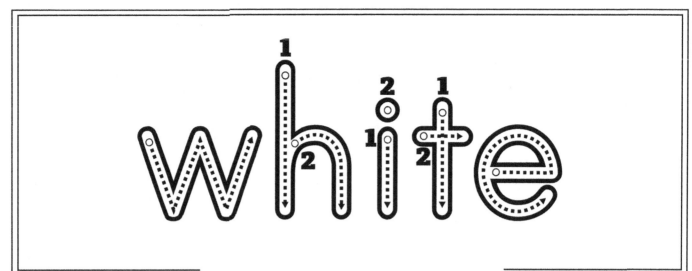

Who Who Who

Who Who Who

Who Who Who

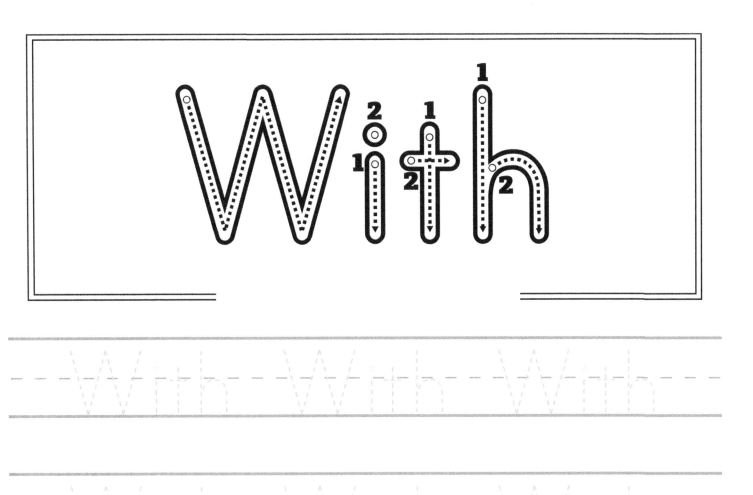

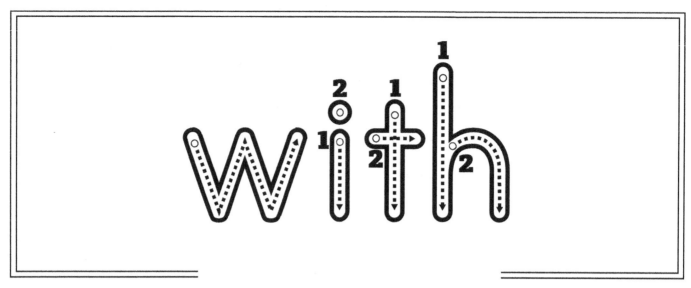

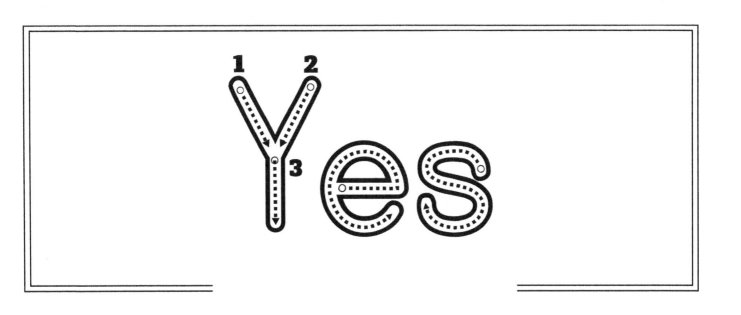

Yes   Yes   Yes   Yes

Yes   Yes   Yes   Yes

Yes   Yes   Yes   Yes

yes

yes   yes   yes   yes

yes   yes   yes   yes

yes   yes   yes   yes

Made in United States
North Haven, CT
10 March 2023

33862262R00070